HOFBURG - VIENNA

Text by: Peter Parenzan

Photographs, lay-out and reproduction, entirely designed and created by the technical deparment of EDITORIAL ESCUDO DE ORO, S.A.

2nd Edition, May 1995

I.S.B.N. 84-378-1270-4

Dep. Legal B. 22323-1995

Editorial Escudo de Oro, S.A.

Heldenplatz and the New Hofburg.

The New Hofburg with the statue of Prince Eugene of Savoy in the foreground.

THE HOFBURG

The Hofburg, the imperial palace, was the home of the Court in Vienna. There is no single façade characteristic of the whole group of buildings, so that at first sight it does not give the impression of having been one of the greatest seats of power in Europe down the centuries.

The distinctive "conche" of the *Neue Burg* ('New Château') was built facing the Heldenplatz ('Heroes Square') in 1913, at the end of the Habsburg monarchy: a show of power that was in fact a thing of the past. The more modest Schweizerhof ('Swiss Court') was the original nucleus of the palace. Here, in 1275, King Otakar extended the fortifications that

Anton Fernkorn: equestrian statue of Prince Eugene of Savoy (raised in 1860-65).

had been begun under the reign of the Babenbergs. Rudolf of Habsburg defeated King Otakar at the Battle of Dürnkrut in 1278 and took over the castle the following year; thenceforth it began to be mentioned in documents as ''castro wiennensi.''

The Hofburg was still a rather modest edifice and a succession of Habsburg monarchs chose not to reside in it. Frederick III lived in *Wiener Neustadt*, the more modern part of Vienna, while Maximilian I preferred Innsbruck. After defeating the Turks in 1529, Ferdinand I decided to transfer his residence definitively from Prague to Vienna. He was responsible for the appearance characteristic of the palace up to the Baroque period: a building made up of four wings with a tower at each corner and surrounded by a moat. Remains of the moat may still be seen in front of the Schweizertor or Swiss Door.

The *Stallburg* ('stables'), the first significant addition to the architecture of the Hofburg, was built in the reign of the Emperor Ferdinand I. It was originally intended to be the residence of his son, Maximilian II. After Ferdinand's death, however, this beautiful building in the classical Renaissance style became the Court stables, whence its name; indeed, to this day it houses the famous Lippizaner horses.

Further extensions were added to the palace in successive centuries, although there was never a unified approach to its architecture: when more space was required, buildings were raised wherever there was room. The financial strictures of the ruling house, due

*Winter-
halter: the
Emperor
Franz
Josef I,
1830-1916.
Oil, 1865.*

Winter-halter: the Empress Elizabeth, 1837-1898. Oil, 1865.

Franz Poledne: the changing of the guard in In der Burg. *Watercolour, circa 1912.*

essentially to incessant wars with the Turks, prevented the construction of a palace worthy of an imperial Court; the buildings remained predominantly fortifications in design for the same reason.

The section that later became known as the Amalienburg was nonetheless built at the beginning of the 17th century, in the reign of Rudolf II (1552-1612), with a view to housing the emperor's valuable collections.

It was not until the time of Leopold I (1640-1705) that a more ambitious plan was undertaken: the construction of the Leopold Wing — *Leopoldiner Trakt* — marked the arrival of the Baroque style for the Hofburg, and in 1667 the emperor was able to set up residence in the new edifice, designed by Martino and Domenico Carlone.

A year later, however, this section was completely burnt down and, despite his chronic financial difficulties, the emperor had to rebuild it: the result was the wing as it stands today. The State apartments, the finest rooms in the palace, are now used as the President of the Republic of Austria's official seat of government.

The full magnificence of the lavish Baroque style was still not manifested at the Hofburg, nonetheless, because in this period the Turks organised a fully-fledged march on Vienna: in 1683 Kara Mustafa besieged the city with an army of 180,000 men. The siege was initially quite successful: despite the impassioned resistance put up by the Viennese, the Turks were able to breach the city's fortifications extensively, particularly around the Hofburg. A com-

The Schweizer-hof, entrance to the Burgkapelle and the Treasury.

Imperial Chancellery Wing: passageway leading to Michaelerplatz.

bined German-Polish army arrived to save Vienna just when it had suffered severe damage and was about to fall into the hands of the Turks: it was liberated on September 12, 1683, by forces led by King John III Sobieski of Poland and under the military command of Charles of Lorraine.

Austria subsequently became a major power thanks very largely to Prince Eugene of Savoy's victories over the Turks, who were still waging war in Hungary.

Leopold I then set about transforming the castle — and seat of government — into a truly palatial residence. To this end he commissioned a great Baroque architect, Johann Lucas von Hildebrandt, to prepare a scale model, but this project was never carried out.

Charles VI (1685-1740) was crowned Emperor in 1711; he was the greatest patron of the Baroque style in Vienna and responsible for the most important such buildings, including the *Karlskirche* (Church of S Charles), designed by Bernhard Fischer von Erlach.

The splendid Imperial Stables were begun in 1719, following plans by Fischer von Erlach the Elder. Their magnificent location, facing the castle, suggests that there was an overall plan to embrace the Hofburg within the Baroque concept of symmetry. Indeed, in 1723, when the Chancellery Wing was built, a new edifice was designed to enclose the whole existing complex, with a Baroque palace in the centre; but this plan was never executed either.

In 1734 Bernhard Fischer von Erlach's son, Josef

Heldenplatz from the Ring.

Michaelerplatz.

Franz Gerasch: the old Burgtheater *in Michaelerplatz. Watercolour, circa 1875.*

Emanuel, designed and built a suitable crowning touch for the palace, facing the *Innere Stadt* or city centre.

But the great rotunda, surmounted by the dome now known as *Michaelerkuppel* (S Michael's Cupola), was not completed until 1889-93. The unfinished building, with the outstanding old *Burgtheater* or court theatre, was the distinctive feature of the imperial palace for 150 years.

Although the Hofburg never attained the splendour of a major palace, two of the buildings making up the whole were completed with all due lavishness and dignity. The Imperial Library was opened in 1726; Bernhard Fischer von Erlach drew up the plans and the paintings are by Daniel Gran. The interior is one of the most impressive, sumptuous Baroque halls ever created in a secular building. Strikingly, the magnificent finishing touches of the Library took precedence over the completion of the Emperor's own living quarters.

The construction of the Winter Riding School was concluded by Fischer von Erlach the Younger in 1733. This superb building provided the ideal setting for performances in which riders displayed their skills on horseback, so highly appreciated in the Baroque era, and was also used as a venue for major operatic productions. In 1743 Maria Theresa celebrated triumph over her enemies by organizing a lavish "carousel of ladies" there.

The Empress Maria Theresa (1717-1780) ascended the throne in 1740. At the outset she was absorbed by wars of succession endangering her reign, so she had neither time nor money to spare for further building works. She had also chosen Schönbrunn Palace as her preferred abode, and devoted her resources to it. Maria Theresa nonetheless intended to harmonize the complex of buildings making up the Hofburg by providing it with a complete series of integrated façades: she commissioned the German architect Balthasar Neumann to submit suitable plans.

The Vienna Boys' Choir.

Once again, however, the ambitious project came to naught due to lack of funds.

In 1741 the old *Ballhaus* — near Michaelerplatz — was converted into a theatre; Josef II renamed it 'National and Court Theatre' in 1776. The building subsequently became known as the *Hofburgtheater* and remained a theatre until 1888, when the New Theatre designed by Semper and Hasenauer was completed, on the Ring. The previous edifice has, however, retained the name *Burgtheater* to this day. Maria Theresa concentrated first on modernising the interior of the Hofburg. She ordered the renovation of the Amalienburg, occupied by Albert, Duke of Saxony-Teschen, who was married to Maria Theresa's daughter the Archduchess Maria Christina. Maria Theresa herself lived in the Leopold Wing, in

the rooms now housing the Presidential Chancellery. Josef II the Reformer (1741-1790) was a thrifty emperor and spent little on the maintenance of his personal court; he even closed parts of the Hofburg which he could not use for any practical purpose. It is thus not surprising that he undertook no rebuilding work to purely formal ends, preferring to promote such socially useful projects as hospitals, universities and workshops.

The turmoil of the Napoleonic Wars did not spare Austria and deprived the Emperor Franz II of the funds required to implement the planned refurbishment and unification of the entire Hofburg.

Franz II (1768-1835) came to power as Holy Roman Emperor in 1792 and abdicated this title in 1806, reigning thereafter as Emperor Franz I of Austria: this

The Burgkapelle.

represented the end of the Hofburg's historical rôle as the administrative seat of the Holy Roman Empire. Despite repeated good intentions, the whole complex subsisted as a motley juxtaposition of styles reflecting six centuries of history.

A new building was added to the ensemble in 1808: a *Festsaal* (banqueting hall) built by Louis Montoyer towards the glacis in the south-west. This neoclassical ceremonial hall, predominantly light yellow, is still one of the most splendid dance halls in the city.

Napoleon occupied Vienna in 1805 and 1809, taking up residence at Schönbrunn. As was his wont, he chose the finest pieces in the imperial collections and removed them to France. The Viennese were really upset, however, by the fact that he blew up the bastions of the Hofburg.

Napoleon's empire was overthrown in 1814; the victors met in the Hofburg for the the Congress of Vienna, in the course of which the boundaries of Europe were reorganized.

Franz I (II), the host, was fully aware of the responsi-

Balthasar Wiegand: view of the Imperial Stables from the outer gate of the Hofburg. Watercolour, circa 1820.

Stallburg, *the stable building.*

bilities of his position: he had the Hofburg and Schön-brunn Palace adapted to the contemporary Empire and Biedermeier styles. The Congress of Vienna gave rise to legendary festivities requiring suitable table-ware; some of this sumptuous material may still be admired in the Collection of Court Porcelain and Silver.

As a result of this congregation of nations, for a while the influence of Vienna, of its arts and crafts, fashion and style, radiated far beyond the frontiers of the Em-pire: during the Congress anyone who, rightly or wrongly, enjoyed repute in Europe had to be in Vienna.

The fact that Napoleon had demolished part of the city's fortifications made it possible to reorganize the lay-out of the buildings on the esplanade in front of the Hofburg.

The public competition to this end was won by the architect P. Nobile, of Trieste: between 1819 and 1824 he built the Heldentor ('Heroes Gate'), the Temple of Theseus and the Corti coffeehouse in the Volksgarten.

The Emperor Franz I (II) was a keen gardener and took a personal interest in the species to be planted in the Hofburg gardens.

Franz Josef (1830-1916) ascended the imperial throne in 1848, at the age of only eighteen, thus beginning the last stage of government by the House of Habsburg-Lorraine. By means of a document writ-ten in his own hand in December 1857, Franz Josef

View of the Volksgarten *(People's Garden), with the*
Theseus Temple and Neue Burg *in the background.*

took the first step in Vienna's transformation into a
capital of historicism: he decreed that what remained
of the ramparts should be razed and the city enlarged. Part of this famous order read as follows: "I re-
quire that the enlargement of the inner city be com-
menced as soon as possible, due provision being
made for its communications with the suburbs, while
also ensuring that the capital of my empire and seat
of the Court be embellished. To this end I authorize
the demolition of the ramparts and the filling-in of
the surrounding moats."

In order to guarantee a high standard of architecture,
the land was sold for considerable sums and the
money paid into the "Vienna City Enlargement
Fund," which — under the sole control of the
Emperor — was then used to finance the building of
monuments.

Initially there was no intention to modify the Hofburg.
The young emperor's mother, the Archduchess
Sophie, nonetheless had the interior decoration
altered, largely in the Rococo and Baroque styles.
This return to tastes of Maria Theresa's period was
in line with contemporary politics: after the defeat
of the 1848 revolution and the restoration of ab-
solute rule, the stylistic features characteristic of this
form of administration at its peak came back into
vogue.

The superb bronze equestrian statues of the Arch-

Anton Fernkorn: equestrian statue of the Archduke Charles (raised in 1853-59).

Redoutensaal *(Ballroom)*.

Ballroom *(Conference Centre)*. ▷

Entrance to the Ballroom — *Conference Centre*. ▷

duke Charles and Prince Eugene of Savoy in the Heldenplatz were created by Anton Dominik Fernkorn between 1855 and 1865. The statue of the Archduke Charles (who was victorious over Napoleon), in particular, with the horse balanced on its hind legs, is considered to be an exceptional demonstration of the sculptor's technical expertise.

Once again — one last time, indeed — the Hofburg's occupants strove to extend and transform the palace by means of a large-scale project of imperial architecture. The original idea was merely to provide adequate accommodation for the emperors' art collections. The site for the new museum was soon de-

cided upon: between the Hofburg and the Court stables.

A number of competitions led to unclear results and heated discussions, so in 1869 Gottfried Semper, a renowned architect and professor from Zurich, was called in to act as arbitrator. Semper originated the idea of creating an ''imperial forum'': connecting the Hofburg to the museums by means of triumphal arches in the fashion of the low antique era, thus raising an architecturally harmonious ensemble.

Semper drew up the plans in conjunction with Hasenauer: ''The main front of the imposing complex was to be presided over by a throne room jut-

Entrance to the Ballroom. ▷

State Apartments: the Emperor Franz Josef's study.

ting out from the Leopold Wing of the old Hofburg and surmounted by the cupola, designed artistically in the shape of a tower. The lateral wings with curved exedrae, whose oval arrangement would be reminiscent of Bernini's colonnade in Rome, and whose architectural design would evoke the colonnade on the east façade of the Louvre, were to be set out in such a way that the focuses of the oval Heldenplatz would coincide with Fernkorn's existing equestrian statues'' (— R. Wagner-Rieger).

Soon afterwards, however, differences of opinion arose between Semper and Hasenauer; the former left Vienna in 1877. Building work on the new wing finally began in 1878. A number of different ar-

chitects continued the project after Hasenauer's death in 1894.

With the advent of Jugendstil (Modern Style or Liberty Style) this kind of monumental building went out of vogue; and the aged Emperor Franz Josef was no longer very interested in rebuilding the Hofburg. The heir to the throne, Archduke Franz Ferdinand, took over the project and decreed that the new design should in no way alter the appearance of the old castle: the idea of a throne room to be built in front of the Leopold Wing thus fell by the wayside.

The building work came to an end with the construction of the *Corps de Logis,* by Ludwig Baumann, in 1907. In 1908 plans to raise a further wing facing the *Volkspark* were abandoned: Semper's concept of an enclosed imperial forum was laid to rest.

In 1916, during the war, the Court administration took delivery of the building, albeit unfinished. At the end of the monarchy, in 1918, the first Republic thus inherited an incomplete imperial forum, the basic concept of which had proved too ambitious for a declining Empire.

The interiors were completed between 1920 and 1926, providing the Republic with reception rooms suitable for all kinds of celebrations and also buildings for use as museums.

The Burggarten, Heldenplatz and Volksgarten

The *Kaisergarten* (later known as the *Burggarten*), *Volksgarten* and *Burgplatz* (later Heldenplatz), between the Hofburg and the Ring, are characterized by the fact that they were not the work of the municipal authorities, but the result of the Emperor's own design. These gardens play an important rôle within the overall lay-out of the Ring, to which they became adapted over the passage of time, since they began to emerge in 1822 and were subsequently extended and altered.

State Apartments: conference room.

State Apartments: the table, laid for dinner, in the Collection of Court Porcelain and Silver.

The Burggarten

This was originally called the *Kaisergarten* — "Emperor's Garden" — for it was intended as the Emperor Franz I's private garden. All the archdukes were required to learn a trade: Franz had chosen gardening, and remained enthusiastically devoted to the pursuit throughout his lifetime.

Because Napoleon had ordered that the Hofburg's fortifications be razed in 1809, and all traces of this humiliation were subsequently eliminated, a number of plans were drawn up for the lay-out of the area that had thus been cleared. The emperor developed his own design in cooperation with Antoine the Elder, the Court gardener: the result was a small garden in the Biedermeier style, every contemporary citizen's ideal. Franz was particularly keen on the adjoining winter garden, where he grew rare species, which attracted great interest at the time. Initially the garden was laid out symmetrically; in later decades, however, particularly under the Emperor Franz Josef, it was gradually changed into a park in the English style. In 1903 the old neoclassical conservatory was replaced by a Jugendstil greenhouse designed by F. Ohmann.

There were repeated attempts to convert the *Burggarten* to the French style, this until in 1914 the following conclusion was reached: "It has fortunately been realized that, given the way the garden has developed, and reorganization would deprive it of the special charm acquired over the years, so it has been decided to leave it largely unaltered."

State Apartments: the main room, with a portrait of the Emperor Franz Josef.

The Volksgarten

Originally — until the incorporation of the suburbs — the city of Vienna was confined to the present-day First District. This small area was densely packed with dwellings, so that there was no room for parks or gardens.

The Emperor Josef II had social concerns: in 1765-66 he opened the Augarten and Prater imperial hunting reserves to the public in order that they might be used for recreational purposes.

Neither park was directly linked to the city itself; as a result, there was no need to take it into account in their lay-out. The landscaping of the glacis area was another significant element. As far back as the 8th October 1770 the Empress Maria Theresa had

ordered that it should be sown ''with clover or other varieties of grass.'' In 1781 Josef II decreed that the municipal authorities should plant trees flanking the pathways. The glacis was thus converted into another recreational zone for the city's population; it soon became a very popular meeting place. Records show that in 1788 a marquee was raised there to serve as a coffee shop, in front of which concerts were held in the evenings. When, in 1817, Franz I proclaimed that Vienna was no longer a stronghold, the site of the former bastion was cleared and set out as garden; the top of the ramparts immediately attracted many citizens. After the demolition of all the fortifications, the nostalgic memory of these leafy walks remained and it took a long time for the newly created parks to make the Viennese

Burggarten: *Palm House, designed by Friedrich Ohmann, circa 1900.*

forget the old pathways on the ramparts. Napoleon's blowing up the bastions in front of the Hofburg in 1809 led to the establishment of the first park in Vienna to be conceived from the outset for the benefit of the people: the creation of the *Volksgarten* marked the beginning of the era of city park planning. Once the demolition of the fortifications had been completed (1816-19), the emperor ordered the simultaneous creation of the *Volksgarten,* the outer *Burgplatz* (now Heldenplatz) and the *Kaisergarten* (now *Burggarten*): a public recreational area, a square for celebrations — also public — and a private garden. Planning the ensemble was entrusted to Ludwig von Remy, but his landscape gardening work

was confined to the *Volksgarten.* All three projects were largely completed by 1825. Antoine the Elder, the Court gardener, had the four lawns in the *Burgplatz* sown in the 1820s; in 1823 F.H. Böckh wrote that they had been ''laid out regularly, not like an English garden, for such gardens were expressly deemed by His Majesty to be unacceptable, since they provide manifest opportunities for mischief and immorality on the part of the populace.''

At a time when the fashion for gardens of romantic design was at its peak, then, this was a park set out on a basis of rectilinear avenues. The central points were two neoclassical buildings by P. Nobile: the Temple of Theseus and the Corti Coffeehouse (part

Burggarten: *statue of the Emperor Franz Josef by J. Benck, 1904.*

of the latter may still be seen in the *Volksgartenkaffee).* Police surveillance was, as mentioned above, an important factor. C.C.L. Hirschfeld, the first major German-speaking authority on gardening, had written of 'people's gardens': "Straight pathways are not only permissible, but in fact preferable, in these cases, because they facilitate supervision by the police, which is often indispensable in such places... The lay-out depends on the specific purpose of the park. People wish to meet, see one another, walk together and converse there. Convenient, rectilinear avenues are better suited to these aims than many winding paths."

The Volksgarten fully lived up to its function as a meeting place: it became the favourite area for the 'beautiful people' of Vienna to congregate. A guide to the city for foreigners, published in 1828, included the following eulogy of the part played by the park: "It is one of the places preferred by refined persons for their leisure... There is a splendid view from this marvellous spot, and no stranger should omit to pay it at least one visit... when the gardens are lit up in the evening, furthermore, he can enjoy their beautiful illumination. In the lower part of the park smoking is prohibited, for the sake of respectability, and so are dogs, due to the disagreeable incidents that have occurred."

The *Volksgarten* was enlarged several times in the course of its history, particularly when the Ring avenue came into being, thus developing into a heterogeneous environment made up of separate, contrasting sections. The garden around the monument to the Empress Elizabeth ("Sissi") was laid out in 1905. This superb statue, one of the most beautiful devoted to the ill-fated empress, is a fitting and secluded culmination of the *Volksgarten's* eighty years of historical development.

Burggarten: *monument to Mozart by Viktor Tilgner, 1896.*

The Hofburg today

As outlined above, the fabric of the Hofburg bears direct testimony to seven hundred years of history of the House of Habsburg and its emperors.

It comprises 18 sections, 54 staircases and 19 courtyards covering an area of 240,000 square metres. This guide will begin in the south-east, with the *Albertina,* describing the various buildings and indicating their present-day uses.

1. *The Albertina*

Albert, Duke of Saxony-Teschen, who was married to Maria Theresa's daughter Maria Christina, commissioned Louis Montoyer (in 1801-04) and Ludwig Kornhäusel (1822) to convert an old palace to the neoclassical style. The building was damaged by bombing in the Second World War; the entrance was subsequently rebuilt, thus altering the main front. Duke Albert's collection of graphic art is still kept, open to the public, in the *Albertina;* the building also houses the Film Museum.

2. *The Albertina Bastion*

This is one of the few remnants of the city's ancient fortifications. The Danube Fountain was sculpted by Johann Meixner, following plans by Moritz von Löhr.

3. *Augustinerkirche*

In the early 14th century the Court church was altered, becoming an edifice made up of a nave and

Volksgar-
ten: *statue
of the
Empress
Elizabeth by
Hans
Bitterlich
and
Friedrich
Ohmann,
1907.*

Ernst Kraner: the Emperor Franz Josef out for a drive. Gouache.

two nave-aisles. The Emperor Josef II had certain Renaissance and Baroque additions removed in 1783: an early instance of restoration of the Gothic style.

Of all the imperial marriages held in the Church of the Augustinians, special mention is due to that of Marie-Louise, daughter of the Emperor Franz II (I), to Napoleon Bonaparte in 1810.

The *Herzgruft* — hearts crypt — was added by order of the Emperor Ferdinand II in 1627: it houses a number of urns containing the hearts of members of the imperial family, as also that of Napoleon's son the Duke of Reichstadt. Their bodies are in sar-cophagi in the *Kaisergruft* at the Capuchins' Church; their entrails, in St Stephen's Cathedral.

Special attention is due to the tomb of the Archduchess Maria Christina, who died in 1798: one of the crowning achievements of neoclassical sculpture, it was the work of Antonio Canova, commissioned in 1805 by the Archduchess's widower Duke Albert of Saxony-Teschen.

4. *The Augustine Monastery*

The monastery of the hermits of St Augustine was founded in 1327. Its library is now part of the National Library (the Augustinians' Reading Room).

Schweizer-
tor *(Swiss
Door),*
1552.

Ballhausplatz: seat of the Federal Chancellery and the Ministry of Foreign Affairs.

5. *The National Library*

This is one of the oldest libraries in the world; it was built by the Baroque architect Johann Bernhard Fischer von Erlach and his son Josef Emanuel in the reign of the Emperor Charles VI. The State Room, 77 m long and 20 m high, is particularly worth a visit.

6. *Ballrooms building*

The Empress Maria Theresa had the Opera Room converted into the Large and Small Ballrooms following plans by Jadot. The first masked balls were held here in 1748. These fine rooms now form part of the Conference Centre.

7. *Stallburg*

This building was raised by order of the Emperor Ferdinand I in 1559; his son Maximilian II had the stables for his riding and carriage horses established there. The New Gallery, on the second storey, is based on a design by the Emperor Charles VI.

8. *Winter Riding School*

The riding arena, measuring 55 m by 18 m, was installed on the site of the emperor's private garden by Fischer von Erlach the Younger, on instructions from the Emperor Charles VI. Its suspended roof is a remarkable technical achievement. There is an inscription describing the functions of the building: "This imperial riding school was built in the year 1735 for the instruction and exercise of young nobles, and also for the training of horses for riding and war, by order of the Emperor Charles VI, son of the former Emperor Leopold I, and under the super-

*The
Presidential
Chancellery.*

Treasure Chamber: the "Potence" (heraldic chain for the herald of the Order of the Golden Fleece, circa 1517).

vision of the director of the building works and of the management committee of the Court stables, Count Gundaker Althann."

The public may now enjoy the famous Lippizaner horses' *haute école* riding performances here.

9. *Michaelertrakt ('St Michael's Wing')*

As far back as the 16th century there was a building used for Court dances and festivities on this site; it was transformed into an opera house by Maria Theresa and into the 'Court and National Theatre' by Josef II. The première of Mozart's opera "The Abduction from the Seraglio," among others, took place here.

The present-day edifice, surmounted by a high octagonal cupola, was raised in 1893 according to plans by Josef Emanuel Fischer von Erlach. Among the many statues adorning it special mention should be made of the groups on the two fountains: "The Power of the Earth," sculpted by E. Hellmer in 1897, and "The Power of the Sea" by R. Weyr, 1895.

10. *Chancellery Wing*

The Emperor Charles VI commissioned Johann Lucas von Hildebrandt to draw up and execute plans for the section of the Hofburg giving onto Schauflergasse. Then as now, it was above all used for office space. The front giving onto the inner square known as "In der Burg" was built by Fischer von Erlach the Younger. The rooms on the first floor, which the Emperor Franz Josef used as his residence, are now open to the public. The room housing the Collection

Rudolf II's crown, later that of the Austrian Empire, Prague, 1602. Imperial orb, Prague, 1612. Sceptre, Prague, 1615. In the background, the Holy Roman emperor's herald's costume.

Coronation robe.

of Court Porcelain and Silver, established in 1893, is reached via the interior of the *Michaelerkuppel* (St Michael's Cupola).

11. *Amalienburg*

This section was built by the Emperor Maximilian II as a residence for his son Rudolf II in 1525. The weather vane on the tower roof is a reminder of the circumstance, for the *Burgrössel* — ''castle knight'' — was the prince's emblem.

The State Apartments of the Empress Elizabeth (1837-98) may now be visited in the Amalienburg.

12. *Leopold Wing*

This was constructed between the Amalienburg and the old Hofburg in 1660, in the Emperor Leopold I's reign. The entire section was rebuilt after a fire in 1681; Maria Theresa occupied the main storey.

These rooms and Josef II's private apartments now house the governmental offices of the President of the Federal Republic of Austria.

13. *Alte Burg*

This — the ''Old Castle'' — was the original nucleus of the Hofburg; the earliest documentary reference, to *castro wiennensi,* dates from 1229. Since then

Cope of the Virgin Mary.

Treasure Chamber: the imperial crown, second half of the 10th century. Imperial orb, circa 1200. Sceptre, first half of the 14th century. Relic of the Holy Cross, post 1350.

Treasure Chamber: cradle of the King of Rome, Napoleon I's son, Paris, 1811.

Corps de Logis *(Ethnology Museum).*

it has been constantly altered and enlarged, retaining nonetheless the appearance of an essentially defensive castle on a quadrilateral ground-plan, with a tower at each corner. All the emperors up to the time of Charles VI, and later Franz II (I) and the Archduke Rudolf, resided in the *Alte Burg.*

Access to the Schweizerhof or Swiss Court and thence the Schatzkammer or Imperial Treasury and the Burgkapelle is via the red Schweizertor (Swiss Door).

14. *Burgkapelle*

The castle chapel was completed in 1449, in the reign of Frederick III, but the interior has undergone repeated modifications. Maximilian I founded the *Hofmusikkapelle* (Court music chapel) and the "Hof-sängerknaben" choir. The tradition continues to this day: the Vienna Boys' Choir performs religious music here at High Mass on Sundays and public holidays.

15. *Neue Burg*

Gottfried Semper and Karl Hasenauer originally (1881-94) planned an imposing imperial forum here; only half of it was actually built. This hemicycle now houses the National Library reading rooms, the Ephesus Museum and the Musical Instruments and Arms and Armour collections of the *Kunsthistorisches Museum* (Museum of Fine Arts). The Ethnology Museum is in the *Corps de Logis* of the *Neue Burg* or New Château.

Museums in the Hofburg

In addition to dwellings, offices of various ad-

Ethnology Museum: Aztec feather headdress, early 16th century.

ministrative departments and the Conference Centre, the expanse of the Hofburg includes a considerable number of museums which visitors to Vienna — each according to his or her own preferences — should not neglect.

Austrian National Library

Collection of Printed Works and Reading Rooms: printed works dating from 1501 to the present day are kept here.
Collection of Manuscripts and Incunabula: readers may consult 38,000 manuscripts, 212,000 autographs and 8,000 incunabula.

Map Collection: comprises 224,000 maps, atlases and 249,000 geographical/topographical sheets.
Music Collection: 45,000 volumes of music, 100,000 pieces of printed music, 64,000 photos and 13,000 records and tapes at the visitor's disposal.
Papyrus Collection: houses 104,000 papyruses, ostraka and parchments.
Portrait Collection and Photographic Archive: 826,000 negatives and 17,000 portraits may be consulted by researchers. The Habsburgs' historic entail library is also administered here.
Theatre Collection: with 1,200,000 autographs, pictures and documents, this is a mine of material for research by academics and laymen.
International Esperanto Museum: founded by

Corps de Logis: *inner courtyard (Ethnology Museum).*

Counsellor Hugo Steiner in 1927, its library now comprises some 19,000 volumes.

Prunksaal (Great Hall): one of the most impressive secular interiors in the Baroque style, open to the public from Monday to Saturday.

Globe Museum: a unique collection of globes dating from the early 16th century to 1850.

Austrian Theatre Museum: specialized exhibitions on theatrical subjects are organized in conjunction with the Theatre Collection.

Albertina Collection of Graphic Art: this is one of the most extensive institutions of its kind, made up of more than 44,000 drawings and approximately 1,500,000 prints.

Kunsthistorisches Museum (Museum of Fine Arts)

Collection of Antiquities in the Neue Burg and *Ephesus Museum:* Greek and Roman finds from the Austrian excavations carried out at Ephesus from 1896 to 1906.

Arms and Armour Collection: founded by the Emperor Frederick III in 1450, this is nowadays one of the most lavish and diverse collections of weapons and armour in Europe.

Collection of Early Musical Instruments: comprising instruments from Renaissance and Baroque royal art cabinets; and others that belonged to Beethoven, Schumann, Brahms, Mahler, etc.

Arms and Armour Collection: suits of parade armour.

Secular and Ecclesiastical Treasuries: this museum displays one of the most valuable treasures in the world, including coronation insignia and jewels of the Holy Roman Empire, the House of Burgundy and the Order of the Golden Fleece. One of the high points in any visit to Vienna.

New Gallery in the Stallburg: masterpieces of world painting and sculpture dating from the 19th and early 20th centuries.

Collection of Court Porcelain and Silver: 18th- and 19th-century articles of tableware from the imperial court.

Ethnology Museum: includes priceless pieces dating from the voyages of discovery of the 16th century.

This institution, embracing practically all non-European peoples and cultures, is considered to be one of the most exhaustive of its kind.

State Apartments: private and official living quarters of the imperial couple Franz Josef and Elizabeth (Sissi).

Spanish Riding School stables: as well as watching the famous Lippizaners' morning exercises, the visitor can view their stables.

Austrian Film Museum: interesting monthly programme shown in the Albertina projection room.

Augustinerkirche - Habsburgs' Hearts Crypt: houses 54 urns containing hearts of members of the Habsburg dynasty.

Arms and
Armour
Collection:
suits of
parade
armour.

FELDKÚRISZ
LUIS, SOHN D. **ANTONIO LEIVA**
/ GEST. 1536 /

National Library: collection of globes.

National Library: details of the Great Hall. ▷

Habsburg Monarchs of Austria

Rudolf I (1218-1291), 1276-1282
Albert I (ca. 1250-1308), 1282-1298
Rudolf III (1281-1307), 1298-1306
Frederick I the Fair (1286-1330), 1306-1330
Albert V (II) (1397-1439), (1404) 1411-1439
Frederick V (III) (1415-1493), 1439-1490
Maximilian I (1459-1519), 1490-1519
Charles V (1500-1558), 1519-1521
Ferdinand I (1503-1564), 1521-1564
Maximilian II (1527-1576), 1564-1576
Rudolf II (1552-1612)

Matthias (1557-1619)
Ferdinand II (1578-1637), 1619-1637
Ferdinand III (1608-1657), 1637-1657
Leopold I (1640-1705), 1657-1705
Josef I (1678-1711), 1705-1711
Charles VI (1685-1740), 1711-1740
Maria Theresa (1717-1780), 1740-1780
Josef II (1741-1790), 1765-1790
Leopold II (1747-1792), 1790-1792
Franz II (I) (1768-1835), 1792-1835
Ferdinand I (1793-1875), 1835-1848
Franz Josef I (1830-1916), 1848-1916
Charles I (1887-1922), 1916-1918

Collection of Court Porcelain and Silver: east Asian china serving vessel, European silver mounting, circa 1740.

Collection of Court Porcelain and Silver: selection of tableware.

Collection of Court Porcelain and Silver: neorococo table service made for the Emperor Franz Josef, Thun-Klösterle, circa 1854.

Collection of Court Porcelain and Silver: cooling receptacles from the Sèvres dinner service, circa 1756.

Collection of Court Porcelain and Silver: chocolate cup, Vienna china factory, circa 1825.

Collection of Court Porcelain and Silver: sugar-bowl and mustard-pot, Ferrier, Antwerp, 1765.

Collection of Court Porcelain and Silver: Milanese centrepiece, circa 1810.

Collection of Court Porcelain and Silver: writing-desk set belonging to the Empress Elizabeth, Franz Jauner, Vienna, 1854.

Collection of Court Porcelain and Silver: decorated plate, Vienna china factory, 1815.

*Collection of Court Porcelain and Silver: decorated
plate, Vienna china factory, 1810.*

Collection of Court Porcelain and Silver: plate with views, Vienna china factory, 1804.

Collection of Court Porcelain and Silver: decorated plate, Vienna china factory, 1815.

Collection of Court Porcelain and Silver: plate with floral motif, Vienna china factory, 1820.

DIE HOFBURG IN WIEN

Baualtersstufen
- Mittelalter
- 16. Jahrhundert
- 17. Jahrhundert
- 18. Jahrhundert
- 1. Hälfte 19. Jahrhundert
- ab 2. Hälfte 19. Jahrhundert

LE PALAIS IMPERIAL DE VIENNE

Périodes de construction
- Moyen-Age
- XVIème siècle
- XVIIème siècle
- XVIIIème siècle
- 1ère moitié du XIXème siècle
- à partir de la 2ème moitié du XIXème siècle

IL PALAZZO IMPERIAL DI VIENNA

Epoche di costruzione
- Medioevo
- '500
- '600
- '700
- Prima metà dell''800
- A partire dalla seconda metà dell''800

THE IMPERIAL PALACE OF VIENNA

Periods of construction
- Middle Ages
- 16th century
- 17th century
- 18th century
- first half of the 19th century
- second half of the 19th century

PALACIO IMPERIAL DE VIENA

Periodos de construcción
- Edad Media
- Siglo XVI
- Siglo XVII
- Siglo XVIII
- 1.ª mitad del siglo XIX
- 2.ª mitad del siglo XIX

SCHAUFLERGASSE

M

10

11

KAISER FR (1)

12

ELISABETH DENKMAL

THESEUSTEMPEL

VOLKSGARTEN

DR. KARL RENNER RING

ERZHG. KARL

0   50   100 m

BURGRING

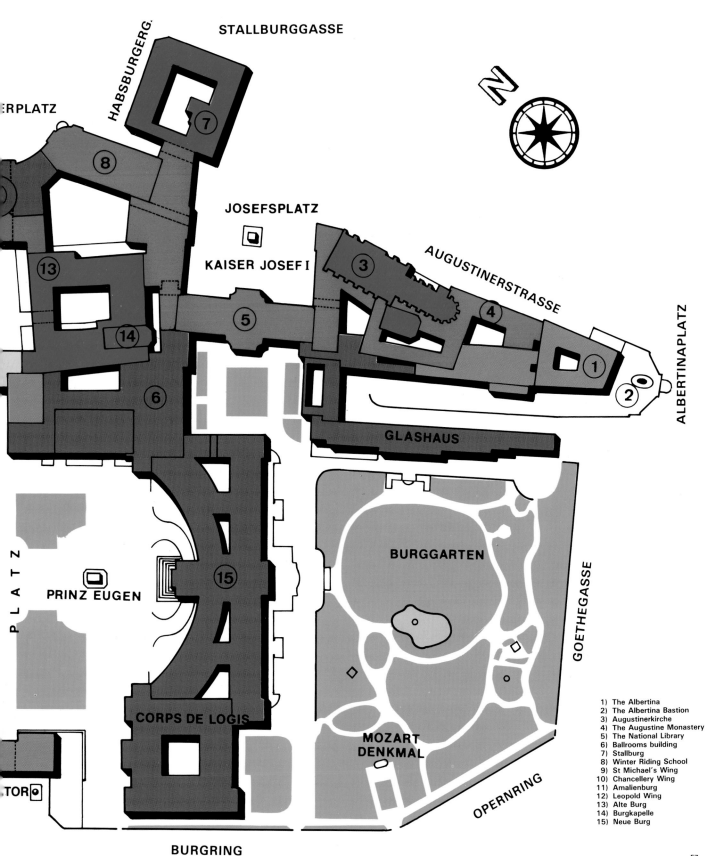

STALLBURGGASSE

HABSBURGERG.

...RPLATZ

⑦

⑧

⑬

JOSEFSPLATZ

KAISER JOSEF I

AUGUSTINERSTRASSE

③

④

⑤

⑭

①

②

ALBERTINAPLATZ

⑥

GLASHAUS

...PLATZ

PRINZ EUGEN

⑮

BURGGARTEN

GOETHEGASSE

CORPS DE LOGIS

MOZART DENKMAL

...TOR

OPERNRING

BURGRING

1) The Albertina
2) The Albertina Bastion
3) Augustinerkirche
4) The Augustine Monastery
5) The National Library
6) Ballrooms building
7) Stallburg
8) Winter Riding School
9) St Michael's Wing
10) Chancellery Wing
11) Amalienburg
12) Leopold Wing
13) Alte Burg
14) Burgkapelle
15) Neue Burg

Collection of Court Porcelain and Silver: Biennais vermeil table service, Paris, 1809 (detail).

Collection of Court Porcelain and Silver: tureen from the Biennais vermeil table service, Paris, 1809.

Collection of Court Porcelain and Silver: gilt silver jug
and serving dish, Johann Biller, Augsburg, 1754.

Cellar: plaster models of sculptures in buildings on the
Ring. ▷

Collection of Court Porcelain and Silver: French
centrepiece, 1851.

Cellar: plaster models and moulds of sculptures in buildings on the Ring.

Collection ALL EUROPE

#	Title	Spanish	French	English	German	Italian	Catalan	Dutch	Swedish	Portuguese	Japanese	Finnish
1	ANDORRA	•	•	•	•	•	•					
2	LISBON	•	•	•	•	•					•	
3	LONDON	•	•	•	•	•						•
4	BRUGES	•	•	•	•	•		•				
5	PARIS	•	•	•	•	•					•	
6	MONACO	•	•	•	•	•						
7	VIENNA	•	•	•	•	•						
11	VERDUN	•	•	•	•			•				
12	THE TOWER OF LONDON	•	•	•								
13	ANTWERP	•	•	•	•			•				
14	WESTMINSTER ABBEY	•	•	•								
15	THE SPANISH RIDING SCHOOL IN VIENNA	•	•	•	•	•						
16	FATIMA	•	•	•	•	•				•		
17	WINDSOR CASTLE	•	•	•	•	•						•
19	COTE D'AZUR	•	•	•	•	•						
22	BRUSSELS	•	•	•	•	•						
23	SCHÖNBRUNN PALACE	•	•	•	•	•						
24	ROUTE OF PORT WINE	•	•	•	•	•				•		
26	HOFBURG PALACE	•	•	•	•							
27	ALSACE	•	•	•	•			•				
31	MALTA		•	•	•	•						
32	PERPIGNAN		•									
33	STRASBOURG	•	•	•	•							
34	MADEIRA + PORTO SANTO		•	•	•					•		
35	CERDAGNE - CAPCIR		•				•					
36	BERLIN	•	•	•	•	•						

Collection ART IN SPAIN

#	Title	Spanish	French	English	German	Italian	Catalan	Dutch	Swedish	Portuguese	Japanese	Finnish
1	PALAU DE LA MUSICA CATALANA	•		•			•					
2	GAUDI	•	•	•	•	•					•	
3	PRADO MUSEUM I (Spanish Painting)	•	•	•	•	•					•	
4	PRADO MUSEUM II (Foreign Painting)	•	•	•	•	•					•	
5	MONASTERY OF GUADALUPE	•										
6	THE CASTLE OF XAVIER	•	•	•							•	
7	THE FINE ARTS MUSEUM OF SEVILLE	•	•	•	•							
8	SPANISH CASTLES	•	•	•								
9	THE CATHEDRALS OF SPAIN	•	•	•	•							
10	THE CATHEDRAL OF GIRONA	•	•	•			•					
11	GRAN TEATRO DEL LICEO	•	•	•			•					
11	EL LICEO ARDE DE NUEVO	•					•					
12	THE CATHEDRAL OF CORDOBA	•	•	•	•							
13	THE CATHEDRAL OF SEVILLE	•	•	•	•							
14	PICASSO	•	•	•	•						•	
15	REALES ALCAZARES (ROYAL PALACE OF SEVILLE)	•	•	•	•							
16	MADRID'S ROYAL PALACE	•	•	•	•							
17	ROYAL MONASTERY OF EL ESCORIAL	•	•	•	•							
18	THE WINES OF CATALONIA	•										
19	THE ALHAMBRA AND THE GENERALIFE	•	•	•	•	•						
20	GRANADA AND THE ALHAMBRA	•	•	•	•							
21	ROYAL ESTATE OF ARANJUEZ	•	•	•	•							
22	ROYAL ESTATE OF EL PARDO	•	•	•	•							
23	ROYAL HOUSES	•	•	•	•							
24	ROYAL PALACE OF SAN ILDEFONSO	•	•	•	•							
25	HOLLY CROSS OF THE VALLE DE LOS CAIDOS	•	•	•	•							
26	OUR LADY OF THE PILLAR OF SARAGOSSA	•	•	•	•							
27	TEMPLE DE LA SAGRADA FAMILIA	•	•	•	•	•						
28	POBLET ABTEI	•	•	•			•					
29	MAJORCA CATHEDRAL	•	•	•	•	•						

Collection ALL SPAIN

#	Title	Spanish	French	English	German	Italian	Catalan	Dutch	Swedish	Portuguese	Japanese	Finnish
1	ALL MADRID	•	•	•	•	•					•	
2	ALL BARCELONA	•	•	•	•	•	•					
3	ALL SEVILLE	•	•	•	•	•						
4	ALL MAJORCA	•	•	•	•	•						
5	ALL THE COSTA BRAVA	•	•	•	•	•						
6	ALL MALAGA and the Costa del Sol	•	•	•	•	•						
7	ALL THE CANARY ISLANDS (Gran Canaria)	•	•	•	•	•			•	•		
8	ALL CORDOBA	•	•	•	•	•					•	
9	ALL GRANADA	•	•	•	•	•		•				
10	ALL VALENCIA	•	•	•	•	•						
11	ALL TOLEDO	•	•	•	•	•						
12	ALL SANTIAGO	•	•	•	•	•						
13	ALL IBIZA and Formentera	•	•	•	•	•						
14	ALL CADIZ and the Costa de la Luz	•	•	•	•	•						
15	ALL MONTSERRAT	•	•	•	•	•						
16	ALL SANTANDER and Cantabria	•	•	•	•	•						
17	ALL THE CANARY ISLANDS II (Tenerife)	•	•	•	•	•			•	•		•
20	ALL BURGOS	•	•	•	•	•						
21	ALL ALICANTE and the Costa Blanca	•	•	•	•	•		•				
22	ALL NAVARRA	•	•	•	•							
23	ALL LERIDA	•	•	•	•	•	•					
24	ALL SEGOVIA	•	•	•	•	•						
25	ALL SARAGOSSA	•	•	•	•	•						
26	ALL SALAMANCA	•	•	•	•	•			•			
27	ALL AVILA	•	•	•	•	•						
28	ALL MINORCA	•	•	•	•	•						
29	ALL SAN SEBASTIAN and Guipúzcoa	•										
30	ALL ASTURIAS	•	•	•								
31	ALL LA CORUNA and the Rías Altas	•	•	•								
32	ALL TARRAGONA	•	•	•	•	•	•	•				
33	ALL MURCIA	•	•	•	•	•						
34	ALL VALLADOLID	•	•	•	•	•						
35	ALL GIRONA	•	•	•	•	•	•					
36	ALL HUESCA	•	•									
37	ALL JAEN	•	•	•	•							
40	ALL CUENCA	•	•	•	•	•						
41	ALL LEON	•	•	•	•	•						
42	ALL PONTEVEDRA, VIGO and the Rías Bajas	•	•	•	•	•						
43	ALL RONDA	•	•	•	•	•	•					
44	ALL SORIA	•		•								
46	ALL EXTREMADURA	•										
47	ALL ANDALUSIA	•	•	•	•	•		•				
52	ALL MORELLA	•	•				•					

Collection ALL AMERICA

#	Title	Spanish	French	English	German	Italian	Catalan	Dutch	Swedish	Portuguese	Japanese	Finnish
1	PUERTO RICO	•		•								
2	SANTO DOMINGO	•		•								
3	QUEBEC			•	•							
4	COSTA RICA	•		•								
5	CARACAS	•										

Collection ALL AFRICA

#	Title	Spanish	French	English	German	Italian	Catalan	Dutch	Swedish	Portuguese	Japanese	Finnish
1	MOROCCO	•	•	•	•							
2	THE SOUTH OF MOROCCO	•	•	•	•	•						
3	TUNISIA			•	•	•						
4	RWANDA	•										

Front cover: Hofburg — Heldenplatz. The New Hofburg is on the right, the Leopold Wing on the left.

Saint Michael Gate by night. ▷